# Worth It

POETRY

## ERIN MATLOCK

ERINMATLOCK.COM

Photography and cover design by Erin Matlock.

ISBN-13: 978-1-7323675-0-0

ATTENTION SCHOOLS, BUSINESSES & ORGANIZATIONS
This book is available at special bulk pricing. Please send an email to
hello@erinmatlock.com for more information.

Set in Prata by Cyreal, Cover set in Nexa Script by Fontfabric, Bodoni
Seventytwo by ITC and IM Fell Flowers by Igino Marini

Publisher's Note: Some names, characteristics, places, and incidents
have been changed to disguise the identities of the individuals involved.
Any resemblance to actual people, living or dead, or to businesses,
companies, events or institutions is completely coincidental and
unintentional.

This book is not intended as a substitute for the medical advice of
physicians and mental health care professionals. Please consult your
personal health care provider in matters relating to your health and
particularly with respect to any symptoms that may require diagnosis or
medical attention.

*For*
*Stephanie Hrna Matlock and Roger Matlock.*
*We made it.*

# Contents

# A New Refuge

They closed in
and grabbed her wings
knowing if they pulled hard enough
they could snap them.

So she kept running
praying with every step
she might be able
to outlast them.

When she finally broke free
of the last tie that bound her
she collapsed
shaken and exhausted.

Carry on my sweet child
it's your stubborn heart
and your wild mind
that will never let them tame you.

And when you wonder
if you will ever again climb that high
your wings may be bruised
but oh do they remember how to fly.

How many chances slip by
in search of perfect
when it is the flaws
of time
of skin
of the world we're in
that give us
our very reason
to begin?

One by one
each petal fell
until what bound us
withered away.

Turns out
those I thought I needed
never planned to stay.

So now I stand
more sure than ever,
I grew strong enough
for the storm
I'm meant to weather.

I starved myself
of my deepest desires
while stuffing myself
with someone else's morals.

The lies
you've been
telling yourself
have become
far too easy
to believe.

There are some
who can stay out all day in the sun
and not get burned.
But the light takes its toll on you.
You reach for it. You bask in it.
Then it becomes too much.
And you know it's time to retreat.
So you rest.
They ask if you're ok. You're fine. You really are.

It's the quiet corner of solitude
that gives you back your peace.

Reminds you that you're strong enough.
Keeps you safe.

You see, the sun was sent
to shine on those who need her.
But you, my dear, are different.

You are the bright, warm light they're seeking.

So have your retreat.
Take your rest.
Listen for the soft voice deep within you.

Your shelter is your rise.
Your power is your love.
And your acceptance of this
is your hard won
freedom.

You have a deeply complex mind that was designed to take you down the winding path of a fulfilled life.

Somewhere in youth we begin to lose our way. As children we are often censored, shamed and taught to look outside of ourselves for validation that we are "good enough" or worthy of approval.

We begin to change for fear of criticism and isolation, and we quickly learn to define our lives by ideals set by power-figures.

The problem is that as you follow guidelines and norms set outside of you, it's easy to lose a true sense of self. You quiet your inner voice and override it so often that you can lose trust in your own choices.

This causes some to veer off the path of alignment and into an upbringing spent pleasing and conforming to others.

And one day, deep into adulthood, you wake up and think to yourself, *"this can't be all there is."*

I asked the mountain
if I was strong enough
to live.
She said
I was weak enough
to love.

I lost my feeling
for everything.
There's no prison cold enough
to describe it.
Dark.
Quiet.
Numb.
Empty.
Could never do it justice.
I wake before the sun
and I climb these mountains
to force myself to feel.
Pain.
Hurt.
Exhaustion.
Joy.
I am terrified
to lose my feeling again.
So I climb and talk to the sky.
Ask questions
and am given answers.
Always.
Whether I'm ready for them or not.

Her voice was quiet
but not weak
slowly sharpening
her knives to speak.

I've always been introverted and shy, and if you're like me then you know we are forced out into a world at a very young age where we are supposed to act like, talk like, and plain old exist like everyone else.

You learn quickly how to toughen up and operate within social confines, but it still takes a toll on your mind, your heart, your entire body.

I could not process what I was feeling and I certainly wasn't old enough to realize I simply functioned differently than my classmates.

So writing became my way out.

It was the one safe place to let my insides outside of me with no fear of disappointing those around me.

It was the undoing of my mind
that gave me back my soul.
I lost her...
somewhere between the foreign lines
of our social confines,
traveling years to learn normal
all the while
letting the best part of me die.

Who knew the untangling of such a tidy knot
would lead to falls down rabbit holes
with crashes to my knees
and the final reckoning with my time.

But I survived.
Surrendered to a force outside of me.
Made a promise I still keep.

From that day I found me,
far from normal
meant for another time.

Here's to the beautiful
undoing of my mind.

3/29/03    MATLOCK

The hardest part of your journey
will be believing in yourself
when there is no reason left to believe.

There are times
when the fear and the pain
are more than your body
was meant to withstand.

You can't breathe.

It's when your heart beats
right through your chest,
and the pounding
is all you can hear.

It's when you're on your knees
at the bottom of the shower,
because your soul is too weak to stand.

And the only thing you can do
is hope that your head
can finally take hold
of your heart
and stop it
from killing you.

This is the reality of living in the storm.

When will the pieces
you've been accepting
no longer be enough?

It happens when you least expect it
often at the most inopportune time
when there are so many reasons
why you can't.

But you must.

You know you have to.
It's the feeling deep in your gut.

The pull.

It's the voice that keeps telling you to do it.

It's called choosing yourself.
*Finally saying yes to what you want.*

Sometimes
the only way
through the fire
is walking
around the fire
and realizing
you don't have to burn.

Loneliness
is your quiet soul
desperate to
remember itself.

What wants you
will hunt you.

How much time
will you spend
waiting for something
that isn't looking for you?

You readied yourself. Gave yourself a pep talk. Hoped that maybe this time might actually work.

You went for it. You had it...the sweet taste of victory. And then without warning it slipped through your hands. *Again.*

There is a saying, "the rejection is the protection." I never liked it, even though it's true. You weren't ready. Or they weren't ready. Either way, it wasn't your match.

When you fall, it's natural to slip into the void of rejection. It's jarring, frustrating, sad.

Remember, that is your guidance. He wasn't the one. She wasn't the one. It wasn't the right time. It wasn't the right company. It wasn't the right position. And on and on and on.

If the guidance didn't feel so bad, you wouldn't recognize it. *It has to feel that bad.* Take the lick. Stand back up. There is so much beauty in the guidance.

You cannot outrun
the pain
that is chasing you.
Let it exist.
Then let it be known
the two of you are done.

The decision you're
refusing to make
is the jagged key
that will leave you free.

Go on and throw your punches
but be sure to aim them at me
for they are far too weak from fighting
and I am your rightful enemy.


Note to Self

If you have come through this life bruised and scarred, I hope you are kind to yourself when you see where you were and where you've come to be.

Life handed you the journey you were meant for even though it's one you never asked for.

Your lessons, brutal as they came, have aged your soul and proven the strength of your spirit.

This life is fleeting, and the mountains are waiting.

Rise up. Speak out. Love hard. Fall down. Get up. Get up. Get back up.

# Heartbreak, My Professor

It is a breath like no other,
the moment just before
you hear your heart shatter.

I fell for the falling. Every time.

Oh how quickly
life becomes a balance
of hanging on by a thread
and reaching for the sun.

Footsteps taken slowly
carve a path of reluctance,
shallow graves left behind
from a now foreign existence.

Belongings sealed in boxes
carry stories we'll surrender,
a once promised lifetime
now only something to remember.

Why does it feel
I must
be less of me
to have
more of you?

Your second home
is not your past.

You wanted him
to want you.
In the end
she won.
Nothing more for you to be,
he simply
was never meant to keep.

How many times
must I choose you
and lose
before I finally learn
to choose myself?

You are the first thought
and the last thought
as I lay down my head
over and over I regret
all
the
things
I never said.

We brutalize
each other's
hearts
trying
to protect
our own.

If you've ever had your heart broken
into a million pieces, then you know
how long it takes to heal.

You know how hard it is to look up
and look out and let anyone back in.

Love is not hard, but it is scary.

To open up to someone and let them
see every flaw, every doubt, every scar
and then hold your breath and hope
that somehow they love you enough to
stick around...that is scary.

To pull your heart out and give it to
someone and hope they don't break
it...that is scary.

To show someone who you truly are
and hope they can still love you in
spite of it...that is scary.

I am lucky enough to have had mad,
wild love in my life. And I am finally
strong        enough        to        accept

that the risk of having my heart
shattered is worth finding that love
again.

I won't tell you I'm steady or
graceful in this. But every day I
wake up, I look up and I look out.

And I tell myself when he shows
up, I will let him in.

You will have it again... mad, wild
love.

Letting go of me
letting go of you
was the hardest freedom
I ever had to choose.

He can not love you
more than he loves himself.

I've had broken bones
splinters and bruises
a concussion
and a coma too
but none ever hurt me as bad
as your I love you.

One by one
I measured them
against you
waiting for the tell.
With my heart unwound
and my mind tied down
one by one
they fell.

We sat side by side on the bed.
Heads dropped. "This isn't working."

We'd moved from hanging on to each other's
every word to avoiding conversation
altogether.

Hoping the silence and the space would
somehow fix us.

For years we'd carried white flags that neither
had the courage to raise.

And so I did for him what I couldn't do for
myself...

I gave him the space to go find her.
Whoever she is. The love of his lifetime.
Even if he doesn't fully believe she exists.

There's something unbelievably cruel about
wanting the best for someone and slowly
realizing you're not it.

To stand by and watch as the light that once lit
up their entire face, slowly fades.

It was heart breaking, but accepting it set me
free.

I tried so hard to lose you
yet I was shocked when I
found you gone.

What I would give for
one last slow dance
with you.

Never did exist
a finer time
than the love we made
inside this mind.

It's a lonely
brand of sad
missing someone
you never had.

I wonder if I could learn to forget you.
Could they erase you from my mind?
A full-on rewind
to the time
when this foolish heart was still wise.

Your cut
taught me
to stitch up
the others.

I have waited far too long
for you to think of me
the way I dream of you.

If I had a daughter
I would tell her I will fail her
time and time again,
but I mean well and I love her
and one day
when she's older she'll understand.


If I had a daughter
I would tell her there are good men.
She'll have to search though,
look inside them, let them grow
and one day
when she meets him she'll truly know.


If I had a daughter
I would tell her
she'll never love the skin she's in.
She need not look
like other girls though
and one day
when she grows up
she'll love herself from within.


I never had a daughter
but I would tell her

I tried so hard
to be a mother.
I spent a lifetime
to fit in.
But I couldn't
and maybe I shouldn't
have ever wanted
to bring her
into this world
I live in.


But I meant well
and I loved her
and one day
when I meet her
maybe she'll forgive.

Promise me you will not
grow so strong
that there is no one left
to be strong enough
for you.

I miss me before you,
and that is how I know.

It's time to search
for what is finding me,
not wait for you to show.

So I will leap.
Arms wide open.
Eyes wide closed.

And one last time,
I will let you go.

# Hold Me Tight

I always wondered
what it would feel like
to have someone
love me forever.

If we search for love
in places it cannot live
we miss in plain sight
the ones meant to give.

They always said
you were lucky
to have me.
Hold on tight
or you'll lose that one.
Even when your last years passed,
your eyes stayed fixed,
your arms wrapped strong.
Who knew in the end
I'd be the lucky one?

Come lay under
the stars with me
and I will draw you
the way home.

Moving on
from holding on
as I finally watch
for someone new
it is the hardest secret
I still keep
that sometimes
I forget to remember you.

She only
wanted him
to love her
the way
she could not
love herself.

Mountains of self doubt
swept out to sea
the minute your lips
pressed against me.

I search for you
in faces I don't know
hoping something about them
will remind me.

One right word
and I can hear you.

One right look
and I can feel you.

I'm slowly gathering pieces
of my familiar.

They say you've been gone long enough
that the things I never told you
shouldn't take
so much
of my mind.

But you were the promise of a different kind.

So lifetimes I will search for you with no shame,
darling I still go weak when I hear your name.

He was a mirror
for who I used to be.
The young me.
The wild me.
Before the first snap of my heart.
And when I looked at him
I came home.

Run away with me
and we will fall
into chaos together.

Looking back now
past the hurt
and the hate
I can finally say
it was an honor
to hold
so much time
in your mind.

He leaned in
pinned my arms over my head.
I knew from first kiss
I could not keep him
but oh the fun of giving in.

I have always felt alone in crowded rooms.

Foreign in my own skin.
Born at an inconvenient time.

A life spent with levels of sadness
no arms were made to hold.

I decided that I would just feel like this
until I could go home.
Maybe next lifetime
things would be different.

I spent decades
running around this planet
searching for love.
Looked everywhere
and to everything outside of me
to fill me with love.

I needed to be loved.

Until one day I woke up and realized...

I am
the very love
I have
been seeking.

You will
never be
too much
for the
right one.

She was
the kind of woman
the stars
wished for,
the sun
set its sights on her,
and the moon
hung on her every word.

He looked at her
heart in his hands
fear in his throat
asking her to love him
believing with all his might
he could be enough.

All this time
I wanted you
to be someone
you weren't.
When I gave in
walked away
and looked back,
I realized
you already were.

He gave her shelter
even though
she didn't deserve it.

Kept watch over her
even though
she wasn't his.

Loved her
even though
she never loved him back.

An unconditional promise
with a bittersweet fate,
it was the wrong lifetime
spent with the right soul mate.

They stared at each other
eyes locked
from across the room.
Two souls who'd spent forever together,
two hearts who'd just met.

I spent a lifetime
not knowing I was lost
until the day I met you
and found me.

Across this bridge
lies peace and belonging
small steps of faith
to a love that is calling.

The first time
you smiled at me
was the last time
this heart was mine.

He looked at me
like nothing else mattered.
I looked at him
like he was the rest of my life.

A thousand lifetimes
could pass me by
and the sun
would never rise
without you
on my mind.

Your love is a legend
let it run fast and free
no worry of abandon
with promise of eternity.

It Was Always You

You are far more powerful
than they have led you to believe.

The takedowns and the knockdowns
are preparing you.

You're getting stronger, braver, wiser.

You're growing tired of the fray.

You have chaos in your soul
and lightning in your veins.

You, my dear, were made
for wild, magical things.

The gravest mistake
one can make
is to doubt the woman
with eyes wide awake.

They stacked
reason after reason
to take flight.

It's too hard
It's too late.
It's not right.

But she stood fierce
under the weight,
repeating
one then another

I'm alright.
I'm alright.
I'm alright.

You are worth
everything
you never knew
you could have.

Some people flow through life
with "nerves of steel."

They think differently, feel differently
and act differently...automatically.

Some of them were born with more resilience.

Others were lucky enough
to learn to become mentally strong
during childhood.

All of them have one thing in common.

These people meet the world on their own terms.

In case they never told you,
you breathe fire.
Eyes wide.
Wings raised.
Now, my child, go slay.

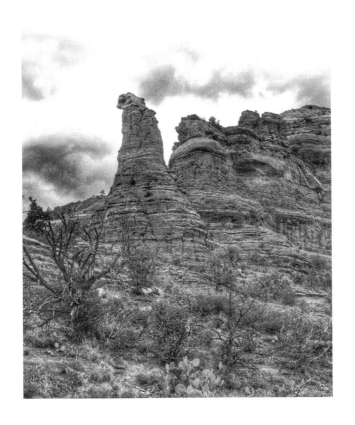

You showed up without warning
wearing your scars
like shiny, new armor.

You threaten them
because you speak your truth.

Stay wild. *They will try to tame
you.*

They'll tell you it's not that
simple. *But it is.*

They'll tell you the storm is
coming. *But it's the darkness that
exposes your light.*

They'll tell you it can't be done.
*But you'll say, "watch me."*

Protect your magic. Trust your
wisdom.

And remember...they are praying
like hell you prove them wrong.

Excuse me
as I break free
of those who confuse me
with who I used to be.

When I see people who fear they are not enough, I see pure hearts. I see inhuman expectations anchored deep in childhood.

I see perfectly flawed beings on the verge of becoming who they were meant to be.

Feeling not good enough, not smart enough, not successful enough...not anything enough...that is your sign.

The untrained eye misses it. Every time.

You are on your beautiful, excruciating path, and it is scary. This, my friend, is how you align.

Speak softly while she dreams
for she breathes fire when she wakes.
She is the bright light rising
and this world shall know her name.

Look up. Everything you want
is already here.

She was the kind of trouble
that burned the stars bright.
The fine taste of freedom
on a fast Friday night.

What someone does
is profound.
How someone looks
is not.

There is a new guard
coming up,
and we are no longer available
for the self-serving dictates
of those self-appointed
keepers of the gate.
We do not fear the fall
for we are united in youth.
Hand in hand we rise,
we are the soldiers of truth.

Look what you've done.
Everything they swore
you could never become.
You had the nerve.
You had the nerve.
You had the nerve
to show them
you were the one.

There are days
when you find yourself
on a roll.
In flow.
Going for something
you never even knew
you could have.
You can taste it...and then there they are.

The ones who take subtle
and not so subtle digs.
The ones who cling to their mediocrity
and try to convince you
that you should too.
The ones who drain you.
The ones who try to ride
your coattails for free.

We're not like that.
We're the kind of people
who remind you
that you breathe fire.

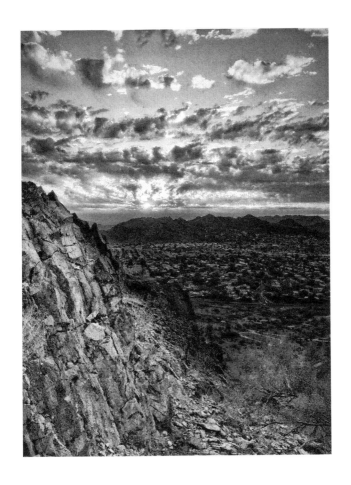

Quiet doesn't mean
                    we don't know the answer.

Quiet doesn't mean
                    we don't know the way.

Quiet doesn't mean
                    we are weak.

It happened again last night. I found myself sitting across from a woman caught in the downward spiral.

We'd seen each other before and had been friendly, but not friends. This was different. She made a beeline for me, took my hand and introduced herself. And I saw it in her eyes...

It's the kind of exhaustion that is easy to hide from everyone else. But if you've been there before, you can always spot it.

I felt like I was looking at myself years ago... scared, sick and desperate for someone to understand me. To help me. To save me.

We talked about things that had worked and things that didn't. We talked about elusive sleep.

She apologized.

Over and over. I used to do the same. You try and fail and fail and fail to simply live like a normal person.

You feel nothing other than worthlessness, burden and defeat. So you begin apologizing for your existence. Mortified you let it get this bad.

But here's the thing... *you didn't.*

You didn't ask for this. You didn't cause this. You didn't make it worse.

You have an illness that can rob you of yourself. It will take everything you used to be...and convince you there's no way left to get it back.

There was a point in our conversation where I saw a shift. It's when the single thread of the impossible knot begins to loosen.

I got a smile out of her...and then there it
was...hope.

I knew she was nowhere near out of the
woods, but when life has robbed you of
yourself, even just a few minutes of hope
are enough to push you through one
more day.

You are the miracle
they never saw coming,
no fire and ice
just slow steady footing.

You've been quietly working
while the rest take the light,
one by one you save them
hiding in plain sight.

Like the stars claim the night
the wild calls your name.
You're the beautiful trouble
they never could tame.

It's not too late.
You're not too old.
You don't need to lose weight.
Your hair is fine.
Yes you can.
The fairy tales were wrong.
No one is coming to save you.
If you don't go after what you want,
no one is going to waltz in
and hand it to you.
So go on now,
it's time you had your own
happily ever after.

You are the fairy tale
they weren't allowed to write.
Stay wild brave child
and shine your bright light.

I hope you remember
the grace of your strength
when the world tells you
you're tattered and worn.
It is the glowing youth
of your heart
and the ageless dreams
of your mind
that have kept you
so beautiful
for all this time.

She wore her chaos
like a sexy black dress
sashaying down the sidewalk
she was life's beautiful mess.

I have failed excruciatingly at times
spectacularly at others,
and I have never once stopped trying
for the fear of failing again.
So carry on my friend,
fail then fail then rise again.

Every crash
into the darkest lows
led to the sweet taste
of the brightest highs,
and even though the rise
was never perfect
every single time
was worth it.

**Erin Matlock** is a writer, artist and globally recognized mindset coach. She is founder of Brain Summit and a dedicated activist and advisor who has spent over a decade in leadership in the brain health, mental health and neurotech markets.

She is an international and TEDx speaker who challenges the stigma of suicide and depression through deeply personal accounts of survival and public recovery.

ERINMATLOCK.COM

# We lose almost one million a year to suicide. I survived.

This is a brutal road to travel, and I want you to know I have been down this same path. *Many times.* I lost 15 years of my life, and I am living, breathing proof that you can survive and manage this illness.

Suicide is still so highly stigmatized, and the isolation and shame are deadly.

You can create a life that brings you love, purpose and happiness. I won't tell you it's easy, but I can tell you that you've already been through the worst part.

Your brain will lie to you and tell you it can't be done. It will tell you that you're a burden, unfixable, broken, weak.

You are none of that. Neither am I.

I will promise you that if you fight, you will win. Not just survive. You must sign up to fight the rest of your life though, and I know you don't have much—if anything—left.

I was there. 4 attempts. 4 lockdowns in psychiatric hospitals. A coma. Life support. Everything I ever had was gone. I could no longer feel. *Anything.* I could not breathe. I saw a monster in the mirror and could not leave my bed for a year.

I gained weight. So much weight I was unrecognizable.

3 pages of medications. Nothing worked until I lay in my hospital bed with my arms and legs strapped down like a wild animal. On a breathing machine with nothing to do but stare at the ceiling.

I made a promise to stay alive no matter how bad life got. It is the hardest promise I have ever made.

My last attempt was a little over 14 years ago.

I function differently than most. I live differently than most. I'm ok with that, because I am alive. I feel again. *Deeply.* Food tastes good again. *Probably too good.* I have times of joy — a feeling I thought I would never get back. I have been in love. Many times. I have friends all over the world — even though I am one heck of an introvert. I am closer to my family than I have ever been. I found work that gives me purpose. And I learned how to tell people no. *A lot.*

I have two talks that people have found helpful. Maybe you or someone you know will find them helpful too.

1) "Changing Fate" - To date the most effective talk I've given on suicide. You are not alone. You are surrounded as we are everywhere. Thank you Jim Kwik and the SuperheroYou organization for your trust on this one.

2) "The Search For A Happier Brain" - A TEDx talk I gave on my initial journey out of traditional depression and suicide treatment, and the steps I took to recover. Thank you Marc Winn and TEDxStPeterPort for bringing me to Guernsey to talk about neuroscience and mental health.

Full length versions of both talks can be found here: erinmatlock.com/speaking

If you or someone you know is dealing with suicidal thoughts, at the time of this printing 1-800-273-TALK provides free and confidential support from trained crisis workers 24 hours a day, 7 days a week.

You can also visit their website if you prefer online chat to a phone call: suicidepreventionlifeline.org

If you are outside of the United States, here is a website which lists international hotlines: suicide.org

Please, please, please. I was a lost cause. Untreatable. I made it. You can make it. – Erin

# Acknowledgments

Krista Sharp for never giving up on me. I would not be alive without your friendship. Michael Sharp for sharing her with me.

To my family and friends who love me no matter what: Ryan Matlock, Yvette Matlock, Adriana and Tyler. Celia Indridson, Daniel Hrna—my Godfather, Kathy Hrna, Daniel Hrna, Anna Marie Smith, Brian Hrna, Penny and Dean Hart, Brandie Rouse, Dorian Morris, Melanie Thomas and Lara White, Peggy Allewell—my Godmother, Annjanette Dasilva, Tiffany Scott, Paxton Allewell, Greg Matlock, Emily and Jared Landry. Hugh, Jean and Michelle. Angela Fuller, Nickie and Donald Knight, Laura Reynoso, Tim Kostynick, Courtney Coady, David Bentzen, Linda Lee McClure.

Christina Rasmussen, what a story we have to tell. Thank you for understanding me. Jim Kwik, for always holding the most magical doors open for me. Marc Winn, my spirit animal. Thank you for your belief and support, and thank you for giving me your TEDxStPeterPort stage to talk about suicide. Alex Doman, Mandy Doman and Ginger Kenney for loyalty and friendship that comes along once in a lifetime. Tori Deaux, for being my fairy godmentor. Jonathan Fields for your uncanny ability to see right through me. Rory Stern, for always, always having my back. Robin Farmanfarmaian for tirelessly supporting the rise of women. Sonia Ricotti for teaching me to go my own way. Andrea Garcia for walking side by side with me through some of the hardest miles of my life…and horsemanship of course. Trudy Scott for your work towards peaceful minds. Max Lugavere for your determination. Sarah McKay for your eternal love of the brain. Drew Ramsey for your dedication to accessible mental health.

Michael Fishman, Elaine Glass and Razi Berry, may we always find friendship and sanctuary in Arizona. Julia Roy for dancing to the wicked beat of your own drum. Cynthia Pasquella Garcia for fighting this fight along side of me. Christi Worsley, Margo Treece, Jamie Pabst, Amy Church Contreras and Liz Porter for welcoming me into your family of service. To Jockathon Pettitt, Jayne Templeton and the very kind people of Guernsey, thank you for opening your arms and your island to an American girl who needed to talk about some difficult things. Tracey Butler, Nacho Arimany, Sheila Allen, Alexis Banc, Debbie Hampton for being very bright sources of love and support.

Kevin Cundiff for always knowing just what to say at exactly the right time. Dan Horner for cheering me on right from the trenches. Max Goldberg for understanding the importance of mental health advocacy. Steven Kotler for introducing me to Mihaly Csikszentmihalyi's work on flow and helping me realize that the mountains were the perfect place to write poetry. Thomas Bahler for making the music play. Clay Hebert for the cocktails and stories we will one day finally share. Melissa Rick for instant, unbreakable bonds. Yvette Roybal for the good you see in everyone. Michael Trainer for your outdoor mind. Denise Larkhin for standing for me when I could not stand for myself. Athena Dorsey Kautz, for showing me that life must be lived now. Elizabeth Meadows and Patsy Graham for taking me under your wings when I was learning to walk again.

John Mekrut, Julie Nelligan, Stuart Silberman, Drema Dial, Patricia Faust, Tina Cufaro, Rachael Dardano, Melissa Wolak, Keira Poulsen, Amber Bloomer, Ellen Goodwin, Adrienne Walker Hoard, Katie Byrne, Kimberly Lukhard, Patti Ernst, Mary Mayotte, Linda Tippett, Gillian Hayes, Tarsh Ashwin, Phyllis Owen, Holly Thompson, Moshe and Adeena Pelberg, Kelly Pittman, Marianne Maes, Tara Hunkin, Andre Duquemin, Melissa Traupmann, Catherine Haskell, Jack Thurston, Yolanda Comparan, Annie Kanjian, Mike Meinke, Pat Quinn, Pat Mattas, Cynde Margritz, Michael Logan, Betty Panarella, Marilyn Abrahamson, Shari Ridge, Rachel Eden, Mischelle O'Neal, Jayne Rutledge, Patricia Roper, Mariam Herrmann, Elizabeth Bailey, Susy Dornberg, Charalampos Chryslkopoulos, Cassandra Herbert, Antoinette St. Clair, Judi Rosenthal, Nancy Freeman, Gaby Urdiales, Marival Gutierrez, Cristina Ruvalcaba Rivera and so many more.

To all the members of The Edge, The Worth It Course, my guest teachers, Brain Summit speakers, colleagues and the private clients who have given me their trust. We are of different faiths, upbringings and edges of the political spectrum, but we hold a space for each other to grow into who we were meant to be. Thank you for being exactly who you are and allowing me to be me.

Jason Johnson, may we always have 90s country and tiramisu. D, for reminding me of who I was when there wasn't a single trace of me left. C, for teaching me that I am beautiful exactly as I am. Kim Crocker, Crissy Herring and Terence Hobbs, we grew up, adulted and all was actually okay. Darryl Johnson and Christina Augustine for loving the stars as much as I do. Madeline and Augustus Johnston for staying true to your dreams, right down to the bone. Bobby Von Jones for your passion to make all women feel beautiful. Lena Vance for so gracefully showing cancer the door. Fred McCall and John Howard for opening your home and your Champagne to me. Brock and John Christie-Hancock, Olivia and Toby for being Zoey's first true friends.

Roxanna Fordon-Seery for your patience and expertise as my therapist.

McG and Z for growing up with me. Mistletoe.

To the therapists, counselors, doctors, nurses, EMTs, police officers, firemen, firewomen, advocates and health professionals who treat the mentally ill with dignity and respect, thank you for fighting so hard to save us.

To the students and staff at Aikin Elementary, thank you for letting me learn how to teach.

To my adopted state of Arizona, it is within your desert valleys and upon your gorgeous mountains that I healed a brutally wounded spirit. This book would not be possible without the gift of your parks and trails.

To Desert Botanical Garden and Bruce Munro Sonoran Light.

To my friends in LaPlace, Louisiana, my brief 5 years with you taught me that family is a state of mind and complete strangers do indeed look after one another.

To Houston, Texas, where I grew up, you continue to show the world that kindness exists even in the darkest storms.

To The University of Texas at Austin, for opening my eyes and my ears to the complexities of this world.

Thank you.

Made in the USA
Columbia, SC
21 September 2018